quiet of chorus

P.O. Box 200340
Brooklyn, NY 11220
upsetpress.org

Established in 2000, UpSet Press is an independent press based in Brooklyn. The original impetus of the press was to upset the status quo through literature. UpSet Press has expanded its mission to promote new work by new authors; the first works, or complete works, of established authors—placing a special emphasis on restoring to print new editions of exceptional texts; and first-time translations of works into English. Overall, UpSet Press endeavors to advance authors' innovative visions, and works that engender new directions in literature.

Cover art by Tracie Cheng / traciecheng.com
Back cover and interior design by Wendy Lee / wendyleedesign.com
Front cover design by Vek Neal

Library of Congress Control Number: 2016941861
ISBN 9781937357979
Printed in the United States of America

contents

i

Whispersound for lost and stolen

Where is the monthly snow, handwritings

of yesterday? Where do the contraband

folds of letter pray? Where have they moved

the fields of killing? Where have they

hidden our angels of embalmment, ceremony

of the dead? Where is the voice each ash

and bone, song of kidnapped ovary? Where

is the thankful one, her memory moon's

old laugh line? Where is exile's red wild

poppy, its blade of grass, its quaking bone?

Notes from the heart preservationist

Hear
tflick
er may no

t come natural each
new. Quiet enough & you to
o may count each be

at—rhyth
m of strange, see
thing body, coll

ected mis
sing. Stil
l—this many

blis
tering summ
ers later. Lo

ok for wa
ter stil
l hugging peri

meter. Its pray
er heavy, this hop
e, tow

n fear. Too, the sag
ging fou
ndation

each nameless
corrid
or. Gravit

y of passe
rsby who wal
k, roll

in sad rhyth
m. Wai
t for the smell

now prog
res
sed to so

ur. Yo
ur body, as mine, mayn't hel
d memo

ry such cut
tings—List
en for lay

ing of trac
k, song
of oocyte's unbo

rn progeny, w
hist
le again

st its undying be
at, presumpt
ion, attempt

s, "reassurance"—
much land brow
n body—

Trains do not stop
now but
to depos

it stran
gers' breath
ren for hiding

behind flower lin
es. Look for the ev
idence, this piece ea

rth: cle
aring of land, drai
ning deposits, fal

se consent for plu
mb line to wea
ther—be

ating of this ama
ranthine heart.

Dear Paradise

so that a returning cloud might carry my tears

—Mahmoud Darwish, "I Belong There"

at someone's imagined creek
crossing
painted on tiles
the shape of tidy
windows,

brights and pastels meet
your spine
room of goodbyes
persistence of synthetic
chairs holding time

this longing to cross
curiosity of flower
line
day
travelers

words we keep
and wait
to sound

The meaning of concertina flower

sacred words ... dressed in lily-white lies

-Marilyn Buck, "Rescue the Word"

Dear Gardener,

Each time   your phantom   breathes

I walk this   unpronounced,

prisoned flower   judas goat

line, your phantom   larynx

limb that prune   time   conjure

and witness   wrinkle coccyx   compass   apostle

unpronounced,   prayer   awaken

each walk

larynx prayer:

may honor

fugitive our

apostle tear,

petition for night sky

in prisons who wish

to gods of this dirt

blacklight yearning

for stars we shine

MEMO

EVERY BONE THIS BODY PRAY YOU NOT MAKE
SPECTACLE THIS HORROR. IT IS NOT BEAUTIFUL.
NOTHING GOSPEL ABOUT BREAKING

BODIES. IT IS NOT BENEVOLENT. NO FESTIVAL
IN TOURISM. DO NOT WRITE TO SHARE LETTERS
AND ANALYZE THE HANDWRITING. DO
NOT VISIT PUBLISH LEAVE AND KEEP STORY

INTACT. COME TO KNOW EACH OTHER LEARN TO
FEED EACH OTHER TOGETHER SUPPLANT THIS

STORM.

ii

Dear Heartprayer Sin,

you pronounce my name
spill prayer, wet gardenroot
chant silent vowel sound

Bodyprayer

Let your skin hold/ the body fall
and footstep tear
na mo guan shi yin pu sa
namo guanshiyin pusa

flesh nimble magnified
anxious/ in dance
Feed this breath/ know this/
heartdrum/ place/

Even if ni wàngjì le/ let
ma's spirit carry you
nã mó guān shì yin pú sà
nãmó Guānshìyin Pú sà

Honor protection ceremony

Driving with the top down sun
out & wind blowing all over the place
xoxo, mm

Trust, child. When
I was 29 & radio
broadcasted "a matter
of principle" we didn't
forecast this

    cloudbreak
         to
    morning onion
        rain: -

        -

        stunned   like the lights

back on before *Where the boys*
    are, someone waits
               for me/ A smilin'
    face—   &   taking off my kitten heels

to throw back
    at the Christopher cops, New Daughters of Bilitis storming

lipstick curls & toothbrushes

angled

at billy clubs   sea a screams pinking   *We*

shall overcome/   *hand in hand*

with the girls

at Gene's, Hair Fairies spilling

onto Taylor & Turk

smoke clouds   like/ *a warm*

embrace,—   two-spirit ghost shirts *knee*

deep   in the earth/

Cover me with pretty

lies/   two arms to hold me

tenderly   from Cambodia fireworks

raining

protractors out a Kent & dogwood blossoms from Cleveland

truck routes/ *where the boys*

are, my true   *love will be*

always my girls & the sons I don't mind callin'

me Dad

Oh, deep in my heart/ & Brother Soledad   *I do believe/*

He's walkin'

down

some street in town and I know he's lookin'

there for me/ In the crowd of a million
    people I'll find/   my fallen

                                    body

Icarus, When Mancusis
ask "Why are they destroying
their homes?" & commissions
write "critical" & "risk
of loss" they did
not risk

        loss
        walking

back from the mess hall/ valentine pulled out a line/ *And then I'll climb*
    t*o the highest   steeple* in this castle
                a towers/ *and tell the world he's*

        mine/ Brother Herb say the world is hearing the world
            is seeing the world
        is coming & the brothers talk to the People of America exploding

guards
    against the walls on fire spreading wild, blowing holes / *'Til*
he holds me
                I wait impatiently/
    Where the boys are, where the boys are morningspark storm
                                    a demons
    / where the boys are

Trust, child. When queens
say "a superb job" &
"tremendous" they did not
see
    Attica is all of us

& I know
    someone waits
for me/ 'Til he holds me I wait

impatiently/ Where the boys are black flowers stemming without
                light or water black that whispers I can't tell you
what the yard was like I cried it was so close everyone together castle
    a flowers thick & bitter/ *where the boys are/ We shall overcome*
these birds a prey firesky deaths
    & stripped naked / *Where the boys are/   We are not afraid*

We are not alone some day/   column a flowers shake shadowmemory

out a hostage echoes knuckled under 'til spirit crawl & beat down
on trouble & trouble plea guilty

/ *some day*   accordion dreams
                              promise

               someone waits for me

                                        I am paper
                              66 & my silvergray wig
               / *hold me tenderly top down where the boys are* sun

       out & wind blowing all over the place/

                              The whole wide world around/ shall
                    overcome
                              their throatslash

                                        some day

Stolen in daylight

despite its dust covering / your shoes

—Elmaz Abinader, "Preparing for Occupation"

Inshallah   you return home
    inshallah   you home whole

  heart still
earth's still quake   the quiet of chorus
             after Gaza
                    sky
                    falling

Borrow/ quick/ the week's groceries/ no
thought/ no recipe
no plan/ but
      hurry.
Before you
leave/ check & check
again/ try & see
the jail color blacklist
Forget the food you
packed/ & door ajar   we sit
        table hips apart   elbow to elbow
      tear tight   this cozy hour
        your hearteye/ refuge
   when jailers descend from uniformed precision stomping
      your face/ steady
        staccato fire ***palestina***

es como el mar   your face/ steady

sixty one years/ collected   raven crowd

aflutter/ **nada**

en el mundo la puede

parar   steady/ of chorus twelve-

year old body/   steady

in prayer

steady/ kaleidoscope rocks of memory

palestina

quiet

es como el mar/ steady sea of chanting

nada   en el mundo

la puede parar

Later find patience/ her still
                    care/ fire phoenix   raven   fly
                                                    brave habibti

                    heart/ keep safe

        still heart/ chant watching/ in days passed
            heart/ quake   *palestina es como el mar*

            Only be your child at home/ inshallah not where wall listen
but heart/ quake
                        slow   *nada en el mundo*
*la puede*heart/ clasp tight   in chance of street & moment meeting
            crowd*parar* the list   妳朋友 who've called/ between
        hidden habibti heart/ your scurried notes.
keep safe

heart/ tear tight

不要看 their black eye camera/ act like strangers in the waiting
area/ Return each call & never

談心丶 on the telephone.

Catch this 秘密/ wider/ than stray ear dare.

heart be

This is how
to keep your terrorist family safe.

palestina es como

el mar/ nada

en el mundo la puede parar

Reconsider your therapist/ this steadfast heart/ keep safe

from watching

heart/ be   heart/ be   heart/ beat that quiet baton

ask what she would do/ if they

came knocking. heart/ beat code of ethics in crumble

palestina es como el mar/   nada en el mundo la puede

parar Remove the battery to whisper sweet dreams and hold her

tight. heart/ chant   heart/ quake

this steadfast heart/ now knowing this missing

the heart

unhemmed/ is capable of crying

Only be

your child at home/ ***palestina es como el mar***

發現到底誰是妳家人/ ***nada en el mundo la puede parar*** Listen

unconditional. 聽 bodymemory

waitbone   tissuesong

heart/ still heart/ push

palestina

es como el mar

heirloom child of silence heart push/ keep safe 妳來

過這裏 inshallah home enough/ to feel

broken./ bodywhisper   threadmovement/ ***nada en el mundo***

la puede parar

skirt

touchmemory/ stillness that lift

edge/ heart

chant   open   crossing

Words we keep and wait to sound

How a seeping spine
understands floodsilence:
"What is this relentless
alphabet of the blameless?
Through the choking blossom
patience of your sandcrown collar
I hear your syllables'
grasping mouth."

Tankasong of kidnapped ovary

(Where one hand cyst
trust) (Where bonerest
hug rupture blood) (Where

egg murmurtomb) (Where
my almond siblinglove) (Where
heartvessel grieve

memorytouch)

letterprayer for child shackle stole

endlessly weavin garments for the moon

-Ntozake Shange,
for colored girls who have considered suicide
when the rainbow is enuf

after star stun night
wondrous fire of yr making
what warm snow bone dusk

still prayin each precious
sand aliveness/ grain of uterus
in grief & bloom

& all i can think is what enormous
blueness/ ocean shaking/ that eldest hands
be outside yr window

iii

Dear Memory Warrior,

amulets against amnesia
-Marilyn Buck, "Rescue the Word"

knees made of fire
breath ceremony travel
imperfect lovely

Breath of Angel Island

No one ever mentions
the curator's selective attentions
or officer's extravagant manner,
barracks of my soundless hum:
columned sleep,
each needless strange suicide,
all the luckless Gold Mountain
compatriots of my anchored shipland.

forego the vanities

first

witch

ancient

hidden

magic hands

burn us

shadow home

for Assata, May 2013

Wardenprayer

To take back such crumpling:
nights now capable

of murder. May afternoon
stolen rest accept these warring

fields of dilemma, almighty
indebtedness to the flawless.

Is this how it sounds to fall?
How quality diminish,

how comfortable silence
missing.

How to follow
the necessary
heart?

Dear Board of Prison Terms,

whisperflash pricks thr

ough your undecided lib

rary stacks/ I have   taken

your   psychological

contrived text;

tests, victim

fences

that

water

impact   &   anger/

management   records

vacant/

Agha

Sha

hid

Ali's

voice

courses

true/

Our memory

history

first sleep

first

the word

then

joy

joy

breath

and slow

soft

smile

first peace

since you

stolen

in daylight

daylight

slow now

less

bright

this wait

something

like child

quiet after

dog well again

home sleeping

first night

this night

door click

room hug you

me quiet

patience

so bright

this slow

breath home

slow

dance

small

step

first time

body

home again

sleep cup you

slow

soft smile

scared

to break again

glimpse of fire

you eye rest my heart

shoulder in fire blink

heat of silent smolder

where body brave sleep

The light we collect

In sleep we sun
medicine light

beneath hours of lost
circadian sky

Outbreath

This mouth of terror
leave no exhale—
million months
military body

groggy eunoia
metonic noctuary

What this piece earth say

Come child, rest your head
Here on my shoulder

Grandmother mountainbreath
Know ocean bloodbreak
Earthmemory know you whole

Here my feet where sheep dream
War homeless, dogma forgotten,
Death that nourish

Valley my breast hold quiet
Spacious enough summer commune
Solitary name unfrozen

Windmemory carry story of ghosts
Who branded yours demonwitches
Broke nieta hands clasped with mine

This porch safe to lay down your pistol
Remove collarmask
Exhale quietpresent

Leaffingers' learned sense

When night return home
Solid blue and perfect as sand
Help carry her starwish doubts

Tuck her in gentle
Sleep by her side

Hear sky lullaby
Silent children of heartbreak
Sound of searise and maple's dying grace

These teardrop rainstories
Splintered bloodroot

In sleep hum patience

When bell of sun wake
And fog lift forestblanket
Kiss night's pillow
Good morning

Walk morning easy
This curve of spine hold
Pressure of whip, cottonwood split

Medicine my scars
Arteries of seed and ash
That mature this love

Walk morning easy child
Come rest on earthshoulder
And the wildness of life

Death's divination, a prison landmemory

Racism ... the state-sanctioned or extralegal production and exploitation of group-differentiated vulnerability to premature death.

-Ruth Wilson Gilmore,
*Golden Gulag: Prisons, Surplus, Crisis,
and Opposition in Globalizing California*

Some call me coffinsea premature prayerbeds.
Each loss resides, spectral trellis.
I hereby make will, revoke what fear
born yesterday's ache, impatience each unlearned lesson.
Bonemarriage null, pursuant order trellis haunting.
The trellisgardener adopted each my million children
and million unborn when starshine needed most.
Tomorrow's beneficiaries, godchildren grief,
executors, will, you, witness.

iv

Dear Sensate Witness,

magic your prayerhands
womb memory's return, wrap
sin, carry new myth

Gaza song

made of nightfall chimes

carried by wind's knowing sigh

sounds from childhood music

box I no longer remember

dancing legacy of Creek and Cherokee stewards

meeting footstep vibration of courage broken

and recovered, seas and lands

away moving and chanting in strong purpose

still believing in life

electric and living

with room to grow old without horror

stars of light

crossing Rafah to tend to Gazans hit by

Israeli sunrise shellings

each broken heart

breathing in prayer to simply live

and love

each desperate inhalation through pillars of smoke

remembering to keep steady through constant groundshake

and the still relentless laughter of evil. I am terrified

to look at another image of sky breaking

open the living

room of someone's home, rockets' fire –

This is not a ribbon dance: this a photograph

of terror I've tried and tried to not reproduce

with words. I want to share

now: menacing strings of fire

festival of lights

grotesquely frozen in time

before streaking down

and down

splintering the middle of a square, behind the basketball hoop

as people bolt under building.

I reconnect with your songstress

winter's winter

hunger for growing blankets of outrage and warmth

to Gaza

and Palestine

and Syria

and Rikers

every living and enduring spirit contained and caught

in unnatural seas of fire

and experience of lockup by lines drawn in greed

onto precious grieving land beneath our swollen feet.

I wish for healing across

generations of bone-broken limbs

and courage-broken hearts

through silence and scream

teachings of elders stolen

across land and sea.

I wish for this healing:

honest

true

full and wide

enough to cover sun

endlessly reflected in sea's unerring mirror.

I wish for you and I stories woven

in cloth from grandmothers' grandmothers' grandmothers.

I wish for exchange of honest feelings

living rooms full of laughter and transformation.

I wish for dances passed through blood

recipes written in our bones

and kitchens full of family spices

we thirst for to carry us home.

Kundiman

of music that wakes us,

—Illya Kaminsky, "Author's Prayer"

If I speak for Melissa I must speak
for L N and youth we do not name
Assata Mumia each name ears have fought to know
Andrea's Osage names stolen inside the chanting
each stolen who's let me hear their heartdrum
each patience in prayer for one kiss with truthsong
all spirits and lovers who carry song without sound
and still dance

Yes I live now the quiet fightdrum
Melissa Melissa Melissa still chanting
You shouted your name for memory still chanting
Melissa far and close still chanting
L N and youth still chanting
each purple flower each return still chanting
Melissa Melissa Melissa still chanting
blank license plate still chanting
Assata Mumia and MOVE still chanting
all hiding in Quezon City still chanting
Melissa far and close still chanting
each who's lost home country still chanting
Andrea's Osage neighbors still chanting
each ghost still not safe to name chanting

Let us be this fightdrum still chanting
each *Kuya, help me* still chanting
each decline to comment still chanting
Melissa's camera memory still chanting
ghost of dead lovers still chanting
showing signs of torture still chanting
medicine for this break still chanting
language evaporate at gunpoint still chanting
stretch and pull each mask still chanting
each door forced open each left ajar still chanting
each stomach caressing ground still chanting
each muscle fight back still chanting
Melissa's *Flame to the Body* still chanting
each *Foot that Bleeds Black* still chanting
each *Incipient Wing that can't fly* still chanting
military gone to hide still chanting
each inch tape each knotted blindfold still chanting
each handcuff's clasp still chanting
temperature their rifles still chanting
each bomb each fire each time still chanting
each death and resurrection still chanting
Melissa's compas inside still chanting

each rib each palm stronger than cages still chanting
each breath you stole for rest each whisper campaign still chanting
each poem speaks later each truthsong before *Night Comes* still chanting
each window sky each freedom found in village arms still chanting
each knowing eye each kind gesture still chanting
each movement til empire fall each rest in love still chanting

gathering this rebel heartdrum still chanting
all this music poetry still chanting

Yes you live Melissa
song of truth rising
your music still chanting

for Melissa Roxas, 2009

Medicine for this break

I love how you
swell
without giving notice, templing
god of we who love
prisoners. I
love your fragile surrender
from blame,
children of grief who
make ego weightless. I
love the hurt
you honor, wondrous gift shaped
by ugly
worship, patient all this time
for one honest
return, freedom, feeling—
like salt
of fear's
sweat, hair
that learn
the charm
of jail
pretense, lid
of each eye
that prolong
tears
begging
forgiveness, blood's prayer
waiting

for moment to rise, each
bone that believes in flutes'
daily practice for the
day our lost and stolen
come home
and we all inhabit
your weathered
body, once unknown
before storm taught love
in release and raised us to
nothing, each rapture a first—and
no regrets.
I love the clarity
in breath,
attention
to your every
motion and still
desire for sweet joy.
May skin breathe,
weary heart
rest and rebuild,
always divine the magic
night's wink.
I love each new day
born of loss,
its silent bruise.
I love the strength
your steady hymn,
harmony to child's
melody for angels.

Poem for California prison hunger strikers

May the hunger
your ghostbody spirit

its prayer
for one photo
and two packages a year

sunlight

food that nourish

and heart
that *experience life*
in the minimum of its meaning—

May stomach anomia
receive what care
each twinge pain
what caress
each dizzying fall

how unknown
this growing nausea
bloom

May bloom enliven
what air long whisper
and breath long brew
how fatigue now sound

louder than *no one*
but the gun tower
can see into

strong enough to cry
a stranger out in chorus

May each forced
swallow psalm
orb
its way out
this windowless sky
eclipsed by incessant star

May ground
that connect you
and me
and each *angry committee*

continue to accept
us in brutal
confusion

and dignity
the sandbag mouth
lift

what hunger sound

*for hunger strikers at Pelican Bay, Corcoran, Tehachapi,
Folsom, Valley State Prison for Women, Centinela, San Quentin,
and RJ Donovan in July 2011*

Desert spiritprayer

At dawn, star's
return above your ground woke
me with sound of wild cats
hungry for shelter,
scorch shortness
jailers' angry ration.

This Friday I pray desert
hymn
through dusk exhaustion
each heavy limb, snakes' torment
confusion, tent's resolve
flapping, flapping.

for Al Naqab prisoners, August 2011

Dear Marilyn,

I heard the storming ululation
in this photograph we reach for
to remember your life by,
soft hearted, still seething,
unprunable in today's cyprus
flame, that still fencing shutter
turned from Lebanon's skyward
village streets, another farewell
dance of rice and roses.

I've never seen a photograph
like this, snapped by a friend
walking prisoned flower line,
courage heart so bare,
so generous, even mums
burst from masqueraded
feeling, each glance reminder
to resist relegation as object
for tomorrow's campaign.

No, we do not mourn you
of loss but in prayer we
may carry on your steel spirit
uncaptured even by the mumstealing
corrosion your jailers' sarcoma.

in memoriam Marilyn Buck, December 13, 1947 – August 3, 2010

Gaza waterprayer

in the clean blue air,

—Mary Oliver, "Wild Geese"

Dear human body,

You do not have to be good or bad.
You do not have to
pray angelic, veil each thousandth
tide this dying
body. You only have to let each
shrivel loosen and
tell what it tells: *fire from the air,*
fire from the sea.
Love me, shrivel to shrivel, as
I've loved each unwanted
red flower. Meanwhile each cell of
child in bodyprayer. Meanwhile
each fold my ocean still swell
awash such jail amassed
through years, the terror each
backlaw bone grown brittle,
dry from such weeping. Meanwhile
the quiet dust sage and cardamom
still speak to the restless ones, wild

now resting in my heart. Meanwhile
we are returning home again.

Whoever you are, no matter
how lonely the trailing paper you

condemn or praise, how ill
the restless imagination, it calls to

you, swimming
my waters, still wild in

love's embrace—over
and over announcing return: simple

prayer each living thing.

in memoriam good spirits of the Mavi Marmara

#OCCUPYCAPITALISM

WE FEEL THE TOXINS WE FEEL THE DANGER

WE HEAR THE CHILDREN WE SEE NO FUTURE

WE BEDBOUND GENDERBOUND JAILBOUND

WE HOMED & UNHOMED WE THIS SACRED FIRE

WE WISH WE COULD GIVE ALL

WE LONGING TO GIVE

WE A CELEBRATION

WE WISH WE KNEW HOW

WE FEEL A TASTE OF IT (FREE)

WE HUNGER LOVE STRONGER

WE SOUNDING THIS LOUDER

WE SMELL A NEW DAWN

WE TASTE THIS NEW POWER

WE STEWARD WE SHELTER

WE SIT WE STAND WE ROLL WE STROLL

WE LIGHT UP OUR BRIDGES

WE LIGHT UP THE SCREENS

WE WITNESS WE PRAY WE GATHER

WE FIND NEW KINDNESS

WE PAUSE

WE KISS THE GROUND

WE SNAKE THROUGH THE CITY

WE MARCH WE CHANT WE MIC WE SIGN

WE LINK ARMS & WE REMEMBER

WE OSCAR GRANT & WE FRANK OGAWA

WE STILL TROY DAVIS

WE SCOTT OLSEN

WE BLEED WE FEED WE WEEP

WE RESPIRE

WE TAKE BACK TO THE STREETS

WE RAW WE TENDER WE SORE ALL OVER

WE CARESS OUR LOVERS

WE FACE NIGHT'S DREAM

WE WORRY WE WITNESS

WE REMEMBER EACH RUPTURE

WE TEND WE MEND WE RECONVERGE

WE BACKLASH BLUE WE NINA'S LANGSTON HUGHES

WE KNEW IMPROVISATION

WE KNEW CHOREOGRAPHY

WE NEW PRACTICE

WE UNDRESS WE UNPOSE

WE NEW HUMILITY WE NEW POWER

WE UNRAVEL WE FULL IN WONDER

WE UNSCHEDULE

WE STILL RITUAL

WE INHALE WE HOLD OUR BREATH

WE KNOW BEAUTY

WE KNOW COURAGE

WE KNOW LEGACY

WE EXHALE

WE KNOW THIS BREATH

WE SKIN WE TINGLE

WE BONE WE MINGLE

WE SONG WE DANCE

WE PRAY WE BODY

WE 1987 WE 1969

WE INTIFADA WE INHERITANCE

WE INVOKE SYLVIA ALIVE AND PRESENT IN THIS SPACE

WE KNOW MAYBE YOU WERE THERE

WE HONOR WHOSE STREETS? OUR STREETS! AND

WE'RE TIRED OF RUNNING!

WE MEMORY WE MUSIC

WE MAKE NEW RHYTHM

WE NEW HORIZON

WE DON'T KNOW OURSELVES

WE ARE LOSING SHAPE

WE STILL HOLD THE RAGE

WE STILL MAKE THE TABLE

WE STILL WATER GARDEN

WE WALK OUR DOG & PUSH THE STROLLER

WE DECIDE WITH STRANGERS & MEET

A THOUSAND NEW NEIGHBORS

WE WAIT FOR FRIENDS WE DON'T KNOW

COMING OUT THE JAIL DOOR

WE WAIT FOR OUR LOVES WHO CAN BRAVE

FLASHBANGS & TEAR GAS

WE TRY TO TUCK OURSELVES TO SLEEP

WE DON'T WANT TO MISS IT

WE WAIT FOR THIS LOVE TO HOME FROM-WITH THE STREETS

WE ARE STILL

WE STILL WHISPER

WE STILL WONDER IF THERE WILL BE A PLACE FOR US

WE LAND IN BODY

WE OCCUPY OUR OWN LONGING

WE REMEMBER THE ISOLATION

WE KNOW EXPLOITATION

WE HOLD ITS SHAPE

WE'VE LEARNED TO CONTAIN IT

WE UNKNOW THIS BODY WITHOUT IT

WE KNOW WE DON'T WANT IT

WE LOSING SHORE

WE CARESS THE TIDE WE CARESS THE BREATH

WE HOLD EACH OTHER

WE ARE CHANGING WE ARE CHANGED

WE SEE MORE OF OUR INVISIBLE SELVES

WE LONG FOR EACH OTHER BUT

WE HAVE NOT REACHED THE HUMAN

WEARING POLICE UNIFORM

WE FEEL OPENED WE STILL PROFIT WE

STILL OWN THINGS BUT

WE CAN TASTE IT

WE WILL LISTEN WE WILL PLAY

WE WILL TREASURE EACH OTHER

WE WILL NOT OUT SOMEONE WITHOUT CONSENT

WE WILL UNKNOW CHILD SEXUAL ABUSE

WE WILL UNKNOW SHAME

WE SEE & FEEL EACH OTHER

WE ARE REMEDY

WE KILL DESPAIR

WE UPHEAVAL

WE'VE RACED OUR HEARTS

WE'VE SURGED THIS SPIRIT

WE RISK & CANNOT RISK & YET WE RISK AGAIN

WE 1946

WE STRIKE THE CLOCK

WE HONOR FIRST NATIONS

WE UNBIND GENDER

WE EVICT TIMEBODY

WE DISABLE "WORK"

WE FREE FROM CAPITAL AND STILL

WE THE BROKEN CHILDREN WHO CRY & WAKE

AND KISS & BREAK

WE RETURN FROM BREAK WE BREAK THE OLD PATTERNS

WE FACE THE FEAR WE FACE THE RAIN

WE RAIN HARDER

WE HEAR EGYPT WE FEEL NYC WE KNOW ATLANTA

WE TAKE DOWN THE FENCES WE REMAKE IT BEAUTY

WE THE WORSHIP WE THE HOUR

WE NOURISH THIS CHURCH WHERE

WE FLUENT LOVE & EASE WHAT FEAR

WE HOLD EACH SACRED WE HOLD THIS SACRED BECAUSE

WE ARE THE ONES WE'VE BEEN WAITING FOR

WE WHO SEE THE POLICE WE NOW ARE BIGGER

WE DON'T AFRAID & WE TAKE PLEASURE

WE WITH BROKEN BACKS & WE WITH BROKEN HEARTS

WE WHO LOST OUR HOMES TO BANKS & BULLDOZERS

WE WHO DID NOT RECOGNIZE THE SETTLERS

WE THE 99% ARE NOT PROTESTING WE RECLAIMING

WE KEEP GOING

WE ARE MOURNING WE THE LAUGHTER

WE IN JUMMA

WE PRECIOUS

WE BREATH

WE HERE

WE OCCUPY-UNOCCUPY-DECOLONIZE 100%

THIS WHOLE BODY

for Oakland General Strike, October 2011

time longer than rope

dancing eyebody
immigrant courage darkest
elegy and return

Landprayer

PROVIDENCE, RI—
Because the wind blows,
releasing a dandelion's
hairs into mating
dance against blue sky.
Because of a mother's
immigrant
determination,
refusal to take no
for an answer
because of english only.
Because birds migrate
to breed, one day
returning
with the season. Because
whales fold the ocean
north to south come
wintertime.
Because pieces of Iowa

sky travel nights
in prayer to recover
her unborn children;
Because rootsilence
patient in sprout,
because soiltruth don't
move, its forest
refuse uprooting
and even grass need
earthbody skyrest.
Because
      horses fly

            for an instant

of time between frames,

and Nehassaiu's flock

no   longer   fly
with   Mother
Hummingbird,.
Quetzal's flight through
the Mission ensnared by
moneyvegan   leather
and   coffee   shops,
along   Manton   Ave
by   downtown's   new
highrise   gracelines
at   night,   and   here

at   foot   of   open
space   between
concertina   wire
and concrete lie

a messy
                row   of   fallen
crows.

Dear Executioners,

If the abolition of slave-manacles
began as a vision of hands without manacles,

—Martín Espada, "Imagine the Angels of Bread"

This the year angels unravel
your promise; enduring prayer hearts
fly home for holidays, stay
for each and all the days,
where bread for all reign free.

This the year no angel
sacrifice your pain, no plea
for life need breath, your swollen
feet return to visit each one
you've put away; this
the year you resolve to face
each sin, confess
humanity with the rest
of us, pilgrims
each and all.

This the year angels
lynched by your pen
and coffee, angels
still keeping
watch inside
return
and bless each memory.

This the year all earth's
children witness
your prison, secrets
broken so no child know shiver
of hunger, shame,
mumstealing, the year each child
remember what it is
to be curious, free from
judgment gaze, relearn
home in body.

This the year we uproot
toxic spread barbed wire
watch tower, pray for each
serving lie
of lock and key; this
the year each immigrant
shriveled under gavel's learned
command lay to rest, medicine
earth's palm massaging
temple our sky, the year new
days rain your wildfire.

This the year strip
searches and forced sterilization
become sorrows
of our past, doctors
and warden find their own
forgiveness enough
to imagine reparation

for war on baby
breath, the year we each find
breath enough
to imagine new
practice, collect
bouquet for each
fallen soldier who
brave this trespass.

If we have learned to hear
prayer of ghosts on Angel Island, then
this is the year; if we felt pollution
from Alcatraz enough to shut
a prison down and dandelion
still root, then
this is the year; if Attica reminds us
that patience shake
foundation enough to threaten
your hold, wake sun
gods, know freedom
for a moment, then
this is the year.

So may each finger's sorrow find
joy enough to loosen your mallet
grip and rest
in prayer
with angels.

Prisonstory

Let us notice the grandeur
prisonstory.
How deep it root, how trim its branch.
What miraging permanence.
This tree of ruin.
Its paging inkwisp, its devotional
spine that shield
such layer in story, tucked
with care so tight
that none can see.

Let us forget ourselves,
the sound of certain,
the fall of city.

How to begin again

And to be carried over
will not be enough—

—Kristine Uyeda,
"Penelope Instructs Her Husband
on the Nature of the Sea"

We emerge, unassuming sailors
of each concrete sea.
We are stolen hearts folded
in half, tucked in the vigil
lines marking each palm's
aging tides, the whisper
of name, the quiet of chorus.
We the patience
in each dull heart
listening for first splintercall
through time's silence.
We the body of refusal demanding
you uncount this numberbody.
We the survival
of generosity singing
prayers for deliverance:
"Grace my falling name."

Manifesto

We believe in home   all home all beautiful   home enough
bellies breathe & sigh   enough skin rest dance free   enough
courage carry all life   this a home no landlord tenant bank
imagine   no passport jail shelter claim   no developer gift no
reparation furnish   this home free a bodycrossing & shame
free a memorybreak   no shame   all beautiful   this home
pray for lost & stolen   home now free a traveling fence
finger & sky breaking open   free enough many home many
body home & whole together   home safe & full spirit prayer
bodyprayer full desire   home wider song & cookin   wider
shape a wood brick & stone   home wider shapes weave
together   full & wide enough spirit return to body   enough
whole body each body heartbody   holy beautiful   holy so
holy body homeless turn home again

We want home   all home all beautiful   home alive so alive
heartbrave thunder shake out a hiding   so holy beautiful & so
holy brave every body home & every body free

for a world without prisons

my abolitionist family and friends

Rose Braz presente!

Notes

"Driving with the top down sun/ out & wind blowing all over the place/ xoxo, mm" is dedicated to Miss Major, from whom the title is borrowed. "knee deep in the earth" and "Cover me with pretty lies" are borrowed from Buffy Sainte-Marie's "Bury My Heart at Wounded Knee." The rest of the italicized text is borrowed from "Where the Boys Are" and "We Shall Overcome." "Where the Boys Are" was the theme song of a 1960 "coming of age" movie about four U.S. college "girls" during spring vacation, and said to be a regular closing night song at the Stonewall. "We Shall Overcome" was the anthem of the Black civil rights movement in the U.S. The poem refers to these resistances: the 1971 rebellion of prisoners at the Attica "Correctional Facility" in New York state, one of whose leaders was Herbert X. Blyden, and where Vincent R. Mancusi was the warden; the three-day 1969 Stonewall Rebellion in New York City, led by two-spirit, transsexual, transgender, lesbian, bisexual, and gay persons of color, at the Stonewall Inn on Christopher Street; Daughters of Bilitis, a lesbian social and political group begun in the 1950s in San Francisco; the Compton's Cafeteria Riot of 1966 in San Francisco's Tenderloin District; the National Front for the Liberation of South Vietnam covertly bombed by the U.S. at its bases in Cambodia; U.S. anti-Viet Nam organizing in the 1970s, including in Ohio at Kent State where students were shot and killed by the National Guard, and in Cleveland, where pictures of the MyLai massacre were first published in *The Plain Dealer*; and the Soledad Brothers – George Jackson, Fleeta Drumgo, and John Clutchette – three Black prisoners at Soledad California state prison defended by Angela Davis.

"stolen in daylight"—"palestina es como el mar / nada en el mundo la puede parar" was borrowed from Latina comrades en route to a January 2009 San Francisco mobilization in response to the Gaza ground invasion.

"forego the vanities" originated as a linocut poem for Assata after the FBI added Assata Shakur to its "Most Wanted Terrorists" list in May 2013, and was written in call and response with Assata's poem, "I believe in living," Audre Lorde's poem "For Assata" (from which "forego the vanities" is borrowed), Lorde's essay "Poetry is not a Luxury," Cheryl Clarke's poem "wearing my cap backwards" (in which she writes, "poets are among the first witches"), and Morgan Bassichis' play "The Witch House."

"Dear Board of Prison Terms," after H. and Agha Shahid Ali's "Farewell."

"glimpse of fire" after S.

"What this piece earth say"— "seed and ash" and "mature this love" borrowed from Peter Forbes and Helen Whybrow; "wildness of life" borrowed from Jesse Maceo Vega-Frey.

"Dear Sensate Witness," after Samara Gaev, from whom the title is borrowed.

"Gaza song"— written November 2012 in call and response with the poetry of June Jordan ("Moving Towards Home"), Suheir Hammad ("Gaza"), Mohja Kahf ("Syria Boxes"), and Rafeef Ziadah ("We teach life, sir"). "relentless laughter of evil" borrowed from June Jordan. "a festival of lights" and "winter within winter" borrowed from Suheir Hammad. "to cover the sun" borrowed from Rafeef Ziadah.

"Kundiman"— after Ruth Forman's "May Peace Come," written as part of a chorus of Kundimans by Asian American poets bearing witness to Melissa Roxas' abduction in the Philippines on May 19, 2009. "Kuya, help me" is from Melissa's affidavit signed May 29, 2009, Quezon City, Philippines. The rest of the italicized text is from a poem Melissa conceived and memorized during her abduction. "each death and resurrection" after "I will learn to Die / a Thousand Times / and Be Resurrected" in Melissa's May 19, 2009 poem. "You shouted your name for memory" borrowed from Ching-In Chen's "Elegy for a Blindfold," also a Kundiman for Melissa.

"medicine for this break"— after Yusef Komunyakaa's "Anodyne."

"Poem for California prison hunger strikers"—"no one but the gun tower can see into" borrowed from a July 2011 letter from hunger strikers at Corcoran's Security Housing Unit in solidarity with hunger strikers at Pelican Bay's Security Housing Unit. "experience life in the minimum of its meaning" and "angry committee" from a hunger striker at Tehachapi's Security Housing Unit.

"Dear Marilyn," after Marilyn Buck's "I Saw Your Picture Today" and a photograph of Marilyn at FCI Dublin taken in 1994 by Mariann G. Wizard.

"Gaza waterprayer"— written following the 2010 BP Gulf Oil Spill. Italicized text from Al Jazeera journalist Jamal Elshayyal, who was aboard the Mavi Marmara during Israel's May 31, 2010 attack on the Mavi Marmara, lead vessel of a Gaza-bound aid fleet, while in international waters. Palestine's Gaza Strip has been under siege since 1967, occupied by Israel until 2005 and since 2007 under Israeli military blockade of basic necessities. "sage and cardamom" references a list of items Israel banned in Gaza.

"#OCCUPYCAPITALISM"— Some text borrowed from and/or response to work and words from Cairo, First Nations elders and leaders, Reina Gossett and Sylvia Rivera Law Project at Occupy Wall Street, Nina Simone, Langston Hughes, Adrienne Maree Brown, Chris Crass, Kenji Liu, Lily Fahsi-Haskell, Mushim Ikeda and the Buddhist Peace Fellowship, and Yashna Maya Padamsee.

"Manifesto"— after Kai Barrow and a campaign and broader organizing in 2009 by the Welfare Warriors and TransJustice in New York City against transphobic discrimination and violence in the city's welfare and shelter systems.

Acknowledgments

To the friends, mentors, and comrades across prison walls with whom I collaborated in decarceration campaigns, movement building, and community organizing in the 2000s, with whom many of these poems grew—especially by way of Californians United for a Responsible Budget; Committee on Women, Population, and the Environment; Creative Interventions; Critical Resistance; Direct Action for Rights and Equality's Behind the Walls Committee; generationFIVE; Justice Now; Transforming Justice; and Transgender, Gender Variant and Intersex Justice Project.

To this collection's earliest readers, Morgan Bassichis, Miss Major, Reina Gossett—thank you for it all.

To the poets and creators of Voices of Our Nation Arts Foundation, Kundiman, and Macondo—thank you for conjuring fellowship at the shorelines.

To Suheir Hammad, Elmaz Abinadar, and Regie Cabico—your witness and teachings were crucial to this work.

To the circle of readers who gave feedback at various stages, and hundreds of individual donors whose belief encouraged this project's completion—thank you. To East Side Arts Alliance and Vimala's Curryblossom Café for hosting call-and-response readings of this work in 2010 and 2012 respectively. The gifts of connection, accountability, and support you each afforded me were invaluable.

To the following publications, where versions and excerpts of poems previously appeared—*Captive Genders: Trans Embodiment and the Prison Industrial Complex* (AK Press, 2011); CounterPunch's Poet's Basement; *Feminist Studies*; *Her Kind*; *Here is a Pen* (Achiote Press, 2009); Fforward Movement: artists in support of the US Social Forum 2010; Marilyn Buck ¡Presente!; OccupyWriters.com, *Poets for Living Waters*; *Taking Freedom Home* (Queers for Economic Justice and Wapinduzi Productions, 2010); *The Revolution Starts at Home* (South End Press, 2011); and *Writing the Walls Down: A Convergence of LGBTQ Voices* (Trans-Genre Press, 2015).

To Minnie Bruce Pratt—thank you for drafting the original notes to "Driving with the top down sun/ out & wind blowing all over the place/ xoxo, mm". To 張世慧老師 at National Taiwan Normal University's Mandarin Training Center—我很感谢您幫助我。

To Zohra Saed and Robert Booras—thank you for blessing this collection with your deep care and partnership; and to Robert for your astute editorial suggestions.

To Cheryl Clarke, for your vital companionship and mentorship, questions and reflection—book revisions and beyond. Thank you for everything.

To my dear Shani and to Lily Fahsi-Haskell, Yvette Choy, and Etobssie Wako for your love and encouragement through this journey. To my friends and families of choice and origin; to my mother, 陳珮; to 毛毛; and to the ancestors—thank you for your supportive presence and insights, near and far, across time and seas. To my father, 黃文亮—thank you for being the first to show me we can envision and build the worlds we need and want.

To the Ohlone, Miwok, Narragansett, Abenaki, Cherokee, and Creek First Nations tribes whose homelands supported me in hearing these poems. To Georgia red clay and California coast redwoods, creekwaters of Walas'-unulstiyi', Pacific ocean edgewaters—thank you.

About Vanessa Huang

Born in Berkeley and home in diaspora from California and Taipei to Atlanta, New York, and Tianjin, Vanessa Huang is a multimedia poet, artist, and cultural worker whose practice inherits teachings from the prison industrial complex abolition, gender liberation, and intersecting social justice movements. Vanessa holds a BA in Ethnic Studies from Brown University, and has worked with racial, economic, and trans/gender justice organizations with a focus on decarceration, homecoming, and transformative justice.

For over 15 years, Vanessa has worked to shift cultural narratives and strategies based in fear, violence, and exploitation towards realities centering love, vision, and transformation. Vanessa has received literary fellowships from Kundiman and Macondo. Vanessa's interdisciplinary work and writings have conversed through community organizing, printmaking, and rallies; film, choreography, and sonic performance; letters to/from prison and with bread delivery through a community supported bakery subscription newsletter; and a range of publications including critical race and gender studies journals, magazines, and scholar-activist anthologies.